# *THE FREEDOM STAIRS*

*The Story of Adam Lowry Rankin,*
*Underground Railroad Conductor*

by
**Marilyn Weymouth Seguin**

## BRANDEN BOOKS
**Boston**

**Library of Congress Cataloging-in-Publication Data**

Seguin, Marilyn.
  The freedom stairs : the story of Adam Lowry Rankin, Under-
ground Railroad conductor / by Marilyn Weymouth Seguin.
      p. cm.
Includes bibliographical references (p.  ) and index.
  ISBN 0-8283-2084-5 (pbk. : alk. paper)
        1. Rankin, Adam Lowry, 1816-1895--Childhood and youth—
           Juvenile literature.
        2. Rankin family--Juvenile literature.
        3. Abolitionists--United States--Biography--Juvenile literature.
        4. Underground railroad--Ohio--Juvenile literature.
        5. Fugitive slaves--Ohio--History--19th century--Juvenile litera-
           ture.
      [1. Rankin, Adam Lowry, 1816-1895--Childhood and youth.
        2. Rankin family.
        3. Abolitionists.
        4. Underground railroad.
        5. Fugitive slaves.]
    I. Title.
E450.R15S44 2004
973.7'115--dc22

2003023778

**B|B**

**BRANDEN BOOKS**
(*A division of Branden Publishing Company*)
PO Box 812094
Wellesley MA 02482

# *Dedication*

The Liberty Monument stands on the bank of the Ohio River in the historic town of Ripley, Ohio. The names of 13 men, including Rev. John Rankin, are carved into the monument as a tribute to their courageous work to end slavery. This book is dedicated to the women and children who also contributed to that effort.

"Ghosts of the past are persistent. Eventually they find a voice and tell their story."—Ardeana Hamlin (*Pink Chimneys*)

# *Table of Contents*

# THE UNDERGROUND RAILWAY

And that bold-hearted yeoman,
Honest and true,
Who, haters of fraud, give to
Labor its due:
Will the sons of such men
Yield to the lords of the south
One brow for the brand,
—For the pad-lock, one mouth?
They cater to tyrants—
They rivet the chain,
Which their fathers smote off,
On the Negro again?

No Never!—one voice,
Like the sound in the cloud,
When the roar of the storm
Waxes loud and more loud,
Wherever the foot of the freeman
Hath prest
From the great River's marge
To the Lake of the West,
On the south going breezes
Shall deepen and grow
Till the land it sweeps
Over shall tremble below!
The voice of a PEOPLE—
Uprisen—awake—
The Western Reserve's watchword,
With freedom at stake,
Thrilling up from each valley
Flung down from each height
OUR COUNTRY AND LIBERTY!
GOD FOR THE RIGHT!
    —John Greenleaf Whittier

*"Running through the dark center of American history there is a vivid red thread of tragedy. Deep in the national subconscious lies the stain put there by the fact that through nearly half of its independent existence the nation had to live with an intolerable thing which could neither be rationally justified nor peacefully disposed of—the institution of human slavery."*—Bruce Catton, in *Reading, Writing and History, American Heritage*, 1956.

# Introduction

The story of the slaves who escaped their bondage is one of the most courageous chapters of American history. Imagine fleeing across swamps and forests with little food or clothing, traveling mainly at night, perhaps to the sound of the baying hounds coming closer with each minute.

Many of the fugitive slave stories were put in writing eventually, and they awakened thousands of readers to the evils of slavery both before and after the Emancipation. One source of these stories is the slave narratives as recorded by 19th century abolitionists; another source is the information collected by the Federal Writer's Project in the 1930s. Together, these accounts give the reader an inkling of what it was like to be a slave, perhaps a fugitive slave.

Most escaping slaves would not have been able to reach freedom without the help of equally courageous men, women and children—black and white—who were willing to defy the law against assisting fugitives, despite the terrible consequences. Ohio's Black Laws made it illegal to give refuge to escaping slaves or to interfere with their capture. In spite of these laws, some individuals began what became known as "the Underground Railroad," which provided the means of escape for thousands. Often, whole families were involved in helping these souls escape, as in the case of the Rev. John and Jean Rankin family of Ripley, Ohio.

Little has been written about Jean Lowry Rankin (indeed, her husband in his autobiography rarely calls her by name, always "my wife"). However, she must have borne the brunt of much of the activity in her household, as Rev. John was often away on business. In addition to feeding and caring for her own 13 youngsters, as well as assorted relatives and students who frequently boarded with the family, Jean Rankin was reported to have sheltered as many as 12 fleeing slaves at a time, and often had to confront angry and dangerous slave hunters.

Consider the responsibility of preparing large quantities of food (without grocery stores), acquiring adequate clothing and supplies for travel (without department stores), attending to hygiene requirements (without indoor plumbing), arranging transportation and connections with other conductors (without telephones or e-mail), as well as caring for her own large family. One source estimates that more than 2,000 slaves came to the Rankin home for help. Reportedly, not one of them was ever betrayed.

This story relates some of the Rankin family's Underground Railroad activity through the voice of Adam Lowry Rankin, called "Lowry," the oldest of the Rankin children. Lowry was 16 in 1832, the year in which most of the events in this story take place. The events are based upon a portion of Lowry's typescript memoir, *Autobiography of Adam Lowry Rankin*, written in the early 1890's, a copy of which can be found in the Union Township Public Library of Ripley, Ohio. When appropriate, Lowry's own words are integrated into these chapters.

*Not infrequently a discussion respecting the quality of horses in the township would wind up with someone saying, 'There are a great many good horses but none is equal to Old Sorrel that raised the Rankin family.' I put this on record in memory of the horse that got me out of so many tight places when working . . . in the Underground Railroad.* (Lowry's Memoir)

# Chapter 1:
# A Narrow Escape

I could tell by the way Old Sorrel's ears were twitching that the slave hunters were close on our trail. I pressed my heels into the horse's side, urging her to go faster. We needed to put some distance between us and the slave hunters if our plan was going to work. When Old Sorrel suddenly picked up speed, I thought I'd lose Ellen, who was holding on to my waist so tightly I could scarcely breathe. As a house slave, Ellen probably had never been on a horse. And now here she was taking a ride for her life!

Beside us, my brothers Calvin and David rode together on Fly. They were grinning. For us Rankin boys, helping slaves escape was high adventure. You better believe that we had a whole bag of tricks for hiding runaways and fooling slave hunters.

The runaway slave Ellen had come to us in the middle of the night, brought to us by a friend who lived close to the Ohio

River that separated the slave state of Kentucky from those of us living in the free state of Ohio.

"This is Ellen. She paid a free Black to ferry her over the Ohio. It's not safe for her to stay long here in Ripley. Her owner already knows she's missing and has most likely already sent out slave hunters to bring her back," said our friend Dr. Alexander Campbell.

There was nothing unusual about this event—Dr. Campbell brought runaways to the Rankin House two, three times a month, especially in the warm months when more were likely to be traveling. Sometimes he brought them to us in the winter too, especially in the very cold months when the Ohio River froze over and the runaways could walk across the ice. My mother provided them for the next leg of their journey with hard bread, cheese, and dried fruit that would not spoil for many days. My father provided them with hope.

Last night as mother gathered supplies for Ellen's journey, Ellen had told us her story. "I nursed mistress's young'un right along with my own Belle, a babe at each breast. When Belle turned 12, she came to work in the big house, right aside me. Mistress, she promised she'd never sell Belle. She's all I had after Belle's Pa was sold down South to work in the fields. Then one day, Mistress up and sold Belle. All she say was massa was takin' a shine to my girl an' she wouldn't have her aroun' no mo'. I vowed I'se done with being a slave or I'se done with this life," said Ellen.

Ellen had been planning her escape for weeks. Her master kept a pair of vicious dogs that he often hired out to owners who needed them for tracking runaways. Ellen had been smart enough to befriend the animals.

"T'was my job to feed the dogs, and I gave them tasty scraps whenever I could sneak 'em from the kitchen. Sho 'nuf, massa sent those old hounds to track me, but dey was racin' far ahead of the massa, and when dey reached me, dey stopped their baying cause I gave 'em pieces of salt pork I took from de pantry. Ole massa must be plenty mad at those hounds."

Her story was not unlike many we Rankins had heard before. Long before any Rankin children were born, our mother, Jean Rankin, and father, the Rev. John Rankin, had declared their war against slavery. Together they vowed to do whatever they could to help those who made it across the Ohio River and needed help in getting to Canada where they would really be free. Father made the escape plans, but it was Mother who supplied the food and clothing for the runaways.

Tonight Mother had prepared a cold meal for Ellen, who had given her own lunch to the dogs, while my sister Isabella packed a small bundle of extra clothing that Ellen would need on her journey. Father gathered me and Calvin and David together so we could plot the next leg of Ellen's journey to freedom. There was no time to waste. If the dogs had failed to track Ellen, then professional slave hunters would be hired to cross the Ohio River to bring her back. There was no shortage of these scoundrels because the reward for returning a runaway in Kentucky was $100—and twice that amount if the slave had crossed the river into Ohio.

"You boys go saddle Old Sorrel and Fly. Take Ellen to Amos Pettijohn—you must get her there before dawn. She'll be safe there until I can arrange her passage," said Father. He turned to Ellen. "I'll arrange passage by boat from Cleveland to Canada. There you will be free forever," he said kindly.

But Ellen was not to be comforted. "My massa will find me, even if I should run to hell, he will find me," she said bitterly.

"Indeed, you had better avoid hell, for you will more likely find your master there than anywhere else," replied Father.

My father was a preacher and a writer who believed in the power of words to make people think—and sometimes, to change their thinking. Powerful speaking was his gift.

"The hardest part is behind you, Ellen. God has been watching over your flight and will be with you until you reach Canada. Put your trust in Him and all will be well."

"Those is kind words. I never got no kind words from the mistress or massa—not one kind word for all the work I done," she said.

So we had left our cozy brick house with Ellen, under cover of the dark spring night. Not a star shone in the sky, and a fine mist sprayed our faces as we rode, making us uncomfortably damp. Soon we came to the fork in the road where we reined our horses to a halt. Behind us we could hear the thundering approach of riders coming fast upon us.

"You know what to do," I said to my brothers as I helped Ellen down off Old Sorrel. Ellen was trembling, but she was quiet. "We'll gain some time when they get to this fork in the road," whispered David. Most slave hunters are none too smart—it'll take them a while to figure out which way to go."

I grabbed Ellen's arm and hurried her into the ditch beside the road. I lay down beside her and we flattened ourselves onto the damp earth. I lifted my head briefly to watch my brothers as they galloped off together into the darkness, David on Old Sorrel, and Calvin on Fly.

"Keep your head down!" I whispered to Ellen. As I pressed my own face into the wet grass, I could feel the vibrations from the hooves of the approaching horses. I could feel the cold dampness soaking though my clothes. It wasn't long before two riders approached the fork in the road and sure enough, they drew to a halt very close to where Ellen and I lay hidden in the ditch.

"Now which way you s'pose they took?" said one of the slave hunters. He was so close to me that I could smell the pungent odor of tobacco, and something sour and foul—urine, perhaps. From atop his horse he sent a stream of tobacco juice our way. I heard the slime land in the grass beside Ellen's head. She never flinched. Maybe she'd fainted—I know I would have done so if I'd been Ellen right then.

"We'll have to split up," growled the other.

"Can't just one of us take on three white men and a runaway," protested Spitter.

"Damn slave stealers—ought to hang 'em, every one—Stealin' a man's property is a crime," said the other. I wondered if he might be Ellen's owner. He jumped off his horse and examined the ground, looking for tracks.

"Looks like they went this way," he said pointing at the road my brothers had indeed taken just a few minutes earlier.

Spitter climbed back on his horse, and just then I heard horses coming towards us on the County Road. That would be my brothers Calvin and David coming toward us, just as if they were heading into town.

"Hey there, you boys seen three white men and a runaway nigger on horseback?" growled Spitter as my brothers came near.

David and Calvin reined to a halt beside the slave hunters. Old Sorrel whickered like she always does when she knows I'm near, but I knew she would never give me away. She knew how this game was played, I'll give her that.

"Sure, we saw 'em. Passed 'em on this road not more'n an hour ago, but they were going at a pretty fast pace," said my brother David. He didn't need to lie to make this trick work. Spitter cursed.

"What you boys doin' out here in the middle of the night anyway?" asked the other, suddenly suspicious.

"Goin' to see Doc Campbell in town. There's an emergency," said Calvin truthfully, for my brothers would indeed report to our father and to Dr. Campbell about the status of our mission.

"Let's go," growled Spitter, and the two slave hunters thundered off along the County Road. Our trick had worked.

When the two riders were out of sight, Ellen and I remounted Old Sorrel. My brothers and Fly headed back home to Ripley as Ellen and I continued on to the home of Amos Pettijohn. Old Sorrel knew the road as well as she did her own pasture. Good thing, cause by now, with the fog and all, I was pretty unsure about where I was. I flapped the reins lightly against Old Sorrel's side.

"Giddap," I urged. She picked up her pace a bit.

Old Sorrel kept on for a few more miles and then stopped abruptly. She whickered and ambled off the road, stopping at a gate, which she nuzzled. Was this the right place? I peered through the fog, trying to recognize the Pettijohn house. What if it was the wrong place?

"Wait here," I whispered to Ellen, and jumped off Old Sorrel, opened the gate and approached the dark house. I rapped the signal on the front window and waited. Three soft raps in rapid succession, then two more. Pretty soon the door opened a crack. Amos Pettijohn stood holding a lantern, the light illuminating my face. When he recognized me, he threw open the door and raised the lantern to cast light on Old Sorrel and her rider. Without a word, he beckoned us inside.

I took leave of Ellen, and I felt good. I had done what I could to help her, and I was sure she would be OK now. No runaway assisted by a Rankin had ever been recaptured. It was time for me to go back home to Ripley. When I mounted Old Sorrel, she tossed her head and whickered. I leaned over her and rested my head against her soft, warm neck.

"Good girl. Good job, sweetie," I murmured. She whickered again. Even a horse needs kind words from its master every now and then.

*A few things in the days of my boyhood were impressed upon my memory: the howling mob that would gather about the little log house my parents occupied and disturb their evening worship of the family; the many drunken men seen in the streets, especially on Saturday . . .(Lowry's Memoir)*

# Chapter 2:
# Rankin Secrets

 My parents moved to Ripley, Ohio when I was five years old. My sister Isabella and my brother David were toddlers then, and that year our brother Calvin was born. Eventually, the Rankin offspring would number nine sons and four daughters. I was named Adam Lowry Rankin, but everyone called me Lowry.

Our first house in Ripley was right on the Ohio River front, and as a child I loved to watch the keelboat drivers navigate the waters. They carried a small mast for sails when the wind was low, and cleats of wood were nailed at regular distances across the deck for the men to press their feet against as they put their shoulders against the end of a long pole set in the sand of the river bottom. Walking from bow to stern, the men thus drove the boat against the stream. I decided that I wanted to build such a boat some day, for I loved the river and I loved working with my hands.

Both my parents had a deep-seated hatred for slavery and vowed to do all they could to end the hateful practice. Some days, Father sat at his desk in the parlor of our Front Street house facing the Ohio River and wrote letters against slavery. He wrote letters to the people of the free states, explaining why they should agree to purchase all the slaves and then free them. He wrote letters to the people of the slave states, explaining why they should agree to free the slaves on those terms. The letters were published in the newspaper.

Every Sunday Father preached against slavery from the pulpit of the Ripley Presbyterian Church of which he was pastor. My father preached that he believed in God who made men and women of many skin colors but all of one blood. He preached that all men and women on earth should reap according to the sweat of the brow, and that those who could not work should pay others to help them. He ended his sermons by saying that all are equal regardless of color. Some of the people agreed with my father, but many others did not. These folks soon stopped coming to my father's church. From an early age, it was clear to me that my father's views on the right way to live weren't popular with all the townsfolk even if we did live in the free state of Ohio.

"Why is it so hard to convince some folks about the evils of slavery, Father?" I asked.

"Some folks believe in law, Lowry. Law says it's all right for one man to own another. But that's man's law, not God's law. If you want to change the way people act, you must first change the way they think."

Father also preached against the evils of strong drink and carousing. In those days, Ripley had plenty of drinking establishments which Father called "doggeries." Saturday nights in Ripley could be pretty lively. It was father's goal to convert the carousers to Presbyterianism and shut down the doggeries once and for all. When Father preached this particular idea on Sundays, he sometimes made more enemies than friends.

Often during our daily family worship, the town rowdies who hated my Father and his ideas, would sneak up upon the house and throw rocks through our windows. One time, when we were at our evening prayers, several men set up a party outside our barn, playing fiddles and drinking whiskey and making so much of a ruckus we could hardly hear ourselves think.

My mother was also an individual of strong belief—and of quick action. My father's words and my mother's acts were spurred by the courage of their shared convictions. It was my mother who placed the lantern in the window each night as a beacon for any runaway who might seek shelter.

The first runaway I remember was Alvin. Couldn't have been more than 20 minutes pass from the time when Alvin came to us before the slave owner knocked loudly on our door, demanding to search our Front Street house.

"I want my property, Rankin," said the man who stood on our porch, beating on our door. While Father stalled for time, Mother hurried Alvin into the room I shared with my brothers. When I sat up in bed, Mother put a finger to her lips and shushed me. In the next bed, my brothers slept soundly.

"We harbor no man's property here," said my father to the man.

We heard a scuffle outside the door, and then the angry voice demanded, louder now for he must have shoved his way past Father and come into our house, "Then surely you'll not object to a search of this house, for I followed the nigra right to your door."

"You may search, but do not disturb my wife and children. There is a sickness in this house," said my father.

I was puzzled by my father's words, for no one was sick in our house. Then I remembered that he and my mother often said slavery was the "sickness of the South."

Mother acted quickly. Pulling the quilt down, she motioned for Alvin to join me in the bed. Then she covered us both, arranging the quilt so that it looked as though one body and not two slept there. Mother sat down on the bed.

"Close your eyes," she whispered. I squeezed them tightly shut. I felt Alvin tremble beside me so violently that the whole bed shook. Then I felt cool air on my face as the slave owner opened the door to my room, and I felt his presence as he approached the bed. I could smell him. I have always been able to smell a slave hunter.

"Surely you would not disturb a sick child," said my mother, and she laid her palm on my brow. I kept my eyes tightly closed and held my breath. Underneath the covers Alvin continued to tremble. And then, so did I.

I heard the slave hunter come closer. I kept my eyes squeezed shut. In the next bed, one of my brothers stirred but made no sound.

"A fever took hold of my household. Surely you'll not want to come much closer," said Mother. She did not have to lie, for indeed a terrible illness had once killed a family that lived in our house. Then I could see light behind my closed eyelids, for the slave owner must have lifted his lantern to shine upon our faces. Finally, he left the room, and then the house, cursing my father.

"You'd better watch yourself, Rankin. We know you harbor runaways here. It's against the law, and one day I'll see you in jail for it."

I wondered who would take care of us if our parents went to jail. I was to worry about this for all my boyhood.

My mother threw back the covers and helped Alvin climb out of my bed. Without a word to me or to my brothers, who were now wide awake and sitting up in their own beds, she hustled Alvin out of the room and closed the door. I never saw Alvin's face, but I had touched him and felt his fear as he lay pressed against at my side, trembling for his life. Although I could have been no more than five or six years old, I sensed that helping Alvin was the right thing to do if my parents were willing to go to jail for it. I knew this without a doubt, for I had heard Father preach that God's law is higher than man's law, and that it is one's moral duty to obey God's law. And even though I was very young, I believed my father's words.

It was Mother's idea that the family should give up the Front Street house.

"But it's a prime spot for our work, Jean. Word's out among the slaves that this house is a safe haven for refugees," protested Father.

"But it's not safe enough, John. The house is too close to the river—slave hunters come right on the heels of the runaways. We need a place away from the river where we can harbor slaves for a time, so they can rest before they journey on," said Mother.

She took Father by the hand and led him to the kitchen window.

"We need to build a house up there," said Mother, and she pointed up at the bluff high above the village of Ripley.

My parents went into debt to buy the land from Mr. Poague, the son of the founder of Ripley. Father hired men to build us a new brick house with an attached summer kitchen. About one hundred feet away from the house, the men built a large barn with stalls for the horses and plenty of room for farm equipment, for we Rankins would have gardens and livestock. Underneath the porch was a roomy cellar for hiding fugitive slaves who could not be concealed inside our house. I have said that my mother was a woman of action.

From the front windows of the new house, we could see a good ten miles of the Ohio Valley. At the foot of the hill lay the town of Ripley, and across the river stretched the cedar hills of Kentucky. The panorama of river, hills and town was magnificent. My mother named our home Liberty Hill. She set my brothers and me to work building a set of stone steps leading from the road up the steep hill to the bluff on which our house stood.

The secret goings on in the Rankin household under cover of darkness sparked adventure and excitement in my boyhood heart. These secret goings on became known as Underground Railroad activity, and our house on Liberty Hill was one of its prime depots. Father was the "ticket master" who made most of the escape arrangements, and Mother was the "station master" who hid the slaves and got them ready for their journey, but it was us Rankin boys who became its chief "conductors" in all of Brown County, and maybe in all of Ohio.

*A Ride for Liberty—The Fugitive Slaves* by Eastman Johnson (courtesy of Brooklyn Museum of Art).

*It was the custom of us not to talk among ourselves about the fugitives lest inadvertently a clue should be obtained of our* modus operandi. *"Another runaway went through at night" was all that would be said.* (Lowry's Memoir)

# Chapter 3: Slave Hunters on the Hill!

Our Underground Railroad activity increased after we moved to Liberty Hill. As I grew older, it became exciting and a challenge for us Rankins to find new ways of hiding the fugitives and of transporting them to the next depot. Although I talked to the fugitives and heard their stories, I knew that I could never truly understand what would drive a human being to take such risks in order to be free.

What did it mean, anyway, to be free? Of course, always having been free, I could never know how awful it must be to live as someone's property. Nor could I really understand the cruelties the slaves spoke of. Having never felt physical suffering caused by another human being, to me their stories were just stories.

And what would happen to the people we'd helped once they reached Canada? How could the fugitives know that life would be any better for them there? Was freedom the absence of pain and suffering? Or was it something else, something so strong and powerful that it could cause a person to leave all that he had known and loved behind and embrace the unknown? Would the reality of freedom be as good as the idea of it?

As a boy, I concentrated on helping fugitives to escape so they would never have to go back to slavery. But father turned his efforts towards preaching emancipation—the immediate freeing of all the slaves. In 1833, Great Britain had ended slavery throughout all the British Empire. Father felt the time had come to do the same in the United States.

"Jean, I have prayed that God would show me a way to spread the word for immediate emancipation. I feel, as you do, that the government should purchase all the slaves and set them free. And He has answered that I must spread the word by traveling to other churches to preach this idea. I believe it is my God given duty to do so," announced Father at dinner one winter night.

And so Father left Ripley to spread the word throughout the state—he was often gone for long stretches at a time. That left Mother and us children to do most of the Underground Railroad work. I agreed with my parents that the slaves should be free, and I wanted to do everything I could to help them get that way. But for the time being, I was content to help those fugitives who showed up at our house on Liberty Hill. Though we'd come close, we'd never been caught at our secret work—not ever.

Of course the fugitives faced a terrible fate if they were caught, for at best, a returned fugitive slave would be sent far south to a lifetime of hard labor in the fields. At worst, he or she could be tortured, crippled, or even killed as an example to the owner's other "property" that running away would not be tolerated. Knowing this, we Rankins were even more determined to help as many fugitives escape as we could. But while my father was away, two things happened that made me realize that the risks we were taking in our Underground Railroad activities were far more serious than I'd imagined.

One day Mother sent David and Calvin with me down the hill into Ripley to the woolen mill to pick up the wool that was given to my father as partial payment of his salary. It was always a delight to my inquisitive mind to be sent on such errands where I could observe the mechanics of a factory. In this case, the woolen mill was driven by a horse walking up an inclined wheel, a mechanism I had once tried to duplicate. The spinning machines, of course, were also of great interest to me, and I had some ideas of how they might be greatly improved.

On this day, my brothers and I were watching the workers spin wool on the "big wheel" into yarn that my mother and her sister, my Aunt Eliza, would weave into blankets and cloth for our clothing. Suddenly, our youngest brother Sam, who couldn't have been more than nine or ten at the time, rushed into the work room, red faced and out of breath.

"Mother says to come quick," he gasped. "Slave hunters are on the hill, and they're armed! They're threatening to search the house!"

I headed for the door.

"Fetch Dr. Campbell and some others. Mother will need the help of armed men," I shouted. "I'll meet you at the house."

My younger brothers took off on foot to enlist the help of friends. My family had no small number of supporters in Ripley, men and women who were willing to take the same risks we did to help escaping slaves—Dr. Alexander Campbell, Thomas and Kitty McCague, Tom Collins. Other friends were free Blacks who acted as guides to escaping slaves seeking the Rankin house—Rhoda Jones, Polly and Lindsey Jackson, Billy Martin and Joseph Settles. It would take some time to alert our friends to the danger on Liberty Hill. In the meantime Mother was facing armed and angry men at the doorstep, with only my youngest brothers and my sisters at the house to help her.

I arrived at our house on Liberty Hill just as the slave hunters were about to break down the door. Mother and Isabella were standing on the porch, trying to stop them.

"Miz Rankin, we followed that slave right to this door. He belongs to me! Open up and let us get him. You've no right taking another man's property. Let us in or we'll knock the door down!" said one of the men. I stepped around the side of the house and faced them.

"Go in and lock the door," I told my mother and sister as I joined them on the porch. But Mother was never one to walk away from a confrontation when she believed she was right. She and Isabella stood beside me, the three of us now blocking the door. The owner of the lost slave came towards us, pistol in hand, followed by seven others, one with a big bowie knife.

"You'll need a warrant to search my house," I said.

"I'm going to search your house now if I have to take your life's blood to do it," growled the man with the pistol. His neck was long and thin, and he bobbed it forward and back like a turkey when he walked. His eyes twitched in anger.

Placing my foot against the house as a brace, I shoved him just as he stepped onto the porch. He took a step back, nearly knocking over his companion with the bowie knife.

"You will do neither," I shouted, but before Turkey Neck could recover from the shove, my brothers David and Calvin, followed by nearly twenty Ripley men led by Dr. Campbell, advanced on the house.

"Just say the word, Lowry, and I will break every bone in his body," said Dr. Campbell, rushing forward with his musket in hand. Turkey Neck looked surprised now, not angry. Clearly he and his men were unprepared to resist my family and the armed men of Ripley.

"That won't be necessary. Let them go," Mother said. The standoff on the porch had lasted long enough. I was sure that if Mother had been hiding a fugitive, he or she would probably be long gone by now. But Mother wasn't finished yet.

"You men are always sneaking around my barn and the yard, pestering me and the children," said Mother to the slave hunters. "Now you get out and get out now, and the next time one of you men shows his face around here, he'll feel the force of powder and shot, and if there's not a man home to do the shooting, I'll tend to it myself!"

Dr. Campbell, and some of the other Ripley men, now stepped forward, muskets pointed at the slave hunters.

"Better get on your horses and go back to Kentucky where you all belong," said Dr. Campbell.

"This woman's got my slave. I followed him straight to her door," Turkey Neck snarled. "I'll be in the house to take back what's mine."

"Then get a search warrant. You can look all you want if you get a search warrant," I said.

But the slave hunters knew that by the time they went back into Ripley for the search warrant, the fugitive would be miles away. Outnumbered and outsmarted, they mounted their horses and headed for the road.

"We'll see you Rankins burned out and all you slave stealing buzzards dead, I swear it!" said one of them as he rode off.

Not a shot had been fired, and I was weak with relief that my family and friends were safe—this time. That episode was the first time I realized that any of us Rankins could be hurt or killed for what we were doing in helping the runaways. But I have said that two things happened to show me what risks my family was taking in our Underground Railroad work.

The second thing that happened was this: We soon got word that a group of Kentucky slave owners had published a reward of $2000 for the abduction or assassination of leading Underground Railroad operators in Ohio, including Dr. Alexander Campbell and the Rev. John Rankin of Ripley.

*Mr. Driscol . . . had implicit confidence in his slaves. He treated them well and often sent them to Ripley on errands. He often boasted that 'no Abolitionist, not even 'Uncle Johnny' (father) whom all niggers like, could persuade my niggers to leave me.' . . . evidently his slaves were not as loyal as Mr. Driscol imagined. They were permitted to go where they chose when their work was done, so they did a large business on the Underground Railroad in Kentucky, helping fugitive slaves and directing them where to go when they crossed the river . . .* (Lowry's Memoir)

# Chapter 4:
# *Rendezvous at the River's Edge*

Because of my father's public views against slavery, slave owners frequently made their way straight to our door when they were looking to "retrieve their property." We Rankins knew some tricks for hiding fugitives—places no slave hunter would think to look. When Father built the barn, he had a false floor put in, making a good sized cellar that could conceal a dozen or more grown adults. We also had a secret basement under the floor of our house, with steps leading down to it from under the floorboards of our back porch. There, Mother stored our winter root vegetables—and hid fugitives when she had to. And we had special hiding places in the woods—caves, coal mines, wood piles where long ago winds had blown over scores of trees, now hollow, that made perfect hiding places. More than once my brothers and I hid fugitive slaves in the coffins built in the workshop of our Front Street neighbor Thomas Collins.

We also knew how to disguise a fugitive so that the slave owner could be looking right at him and still not know his "property" was in his very presence. One time we hid a young woman in a corn shock for more than an hour while her master searched our house and outbuildings. Another time we hid an entire family in a hollowed-out space in our woodpile right next to the house.

Sometimes we had to devise secret signals so that those we had hidden would know when it was safe to move on or whether they should stay concealed. An overturned bucket, for example, set upon the porch, might tell a hidden slave that a bounty hunter had been spotted in Ripley. We also learned to talk in a code that only we Rankins understood, even though we could speak the words in front of others. When Mother told me in the winter to "throw a horse-blanket over the pump to keep the handle from freezing overnight," I understood her to mean that the Ohio River now had a coat of ice thick enough to support the weight of a man, and that we might expect a runaway crossing the river from Kentucky. We referred to our Underground Railroad work as "the business of Egypt."

We always had to think of new disguises and new hiding places, for once a person was in a place, he left his imprint, and there were plenty of slave hunters who were very good at finding those traces. A path through the woods made by as few as two people treading on it left an imprint on the earth. Paths and hiding places could seldom be used again for that reason. So we Rankins were always talking and plotting, and getting ready to welcome the next fugitive on the way to freedom because we believed that all the runaways who came to us for help left their imprint on our lives, just as their feet left an imprint upon the earth.

Although we were a large family, we couldn't do our secretive work alone. Sometimes help came from unexpected sources. One day my father sent me on an errand to the riverfront to fetch a load of lumber to be used for a new addition on the church. I pulled my wagon into the lumberyard. I signed the bill of sale for the lumber and began loading it onto the wagon.

"I can help you, sir?" said a voice behind me. A very dark skinned young man about my own age stood by the wagon. Without waiting for my answer, he began to help me load the lumber I had just purchased onto the wagon.

"You work here?" I asked, thinking him to be one of the free Blacks who lived nearby.

"No sir. I be Sam, the property of Mr. Peter Driscol."

I knew Mr. Driscol lived just above the town on the Kentucky side of the river. He owned many slaves and apparently treated them well enough I'd heard. Still, bondage is bondage. I looked around the lumberyard, but I didn't see Mr. Driscol.

"I'm Lowry Rankin. What's your business here?" I asked just to be friendly and start some conversation. It was sweltering in the lumberyard, and I was glad for some company to keep my mind off how miserable I was.

"I'm here to fetch lumber, same's you," he answered.

The sun beat down, and our sweat drenched us as we worked. When we had finished loading my wagon, I offered to help Sam with his load. There was still no sign of Mr. Driscol.

"Massa sent me here by myself. I'se to fetch the lumber and be home fo' dark. Mr. Driscol never comes with me when I come to Ripley," said Sam.

"Then why don't you stay? Ohio is a free state, and there are people here who could help you go to Canada where you'd be free forever," I said.

"I'd sooner see the moon fall than run away from Massa Driscol," said Sam as we loaded the last of the lumber onto his wagon. "All his nigras feel the same."

Sam's words troubled me for I'd believed all slaves would choose to be free if they could be. I drove my load of lumber to the church where my brothers helped me to unload it.

Two days later, Father got word that three runaway slaves, a man and two boys, were hiding in the woods on the Kentucky side of the river waiting for passage across the Ohio. Father had received word that at about midnight the fugitives would be transported to the Ohio side of the river where I was to meet them and take them on to Red Oak. I left the house well before midnight. The night was warm. There was a half moon and scattered clouds. I hitched Old Sorrel to one of our wagons that I had redesigned so that it had a false bottom. Two boys could easily hide in the secret space I'd built there. I tossed a pile of hay into the wagon bed. The man would have to conceal himself in the hay once I'd hidden the boys under the false bottom.

I drove the wagon to an isolated spot on the riverfront and waited. It was very quiet. Old Sorrel whickered and dropped her head to nibble at the grass. I drowsed in the warmth of the quiet August night. A dog howled in the distance. How I had wished for a dog when I was a boy. But a barking dog would be no friend of the Rankins, for those who skulked around Liberty Hill at night could be either friend or foe, and a dog would make no distinction. The Rankins owned not even a hunting dog.

Maybe twenty minutes passed, maybe an hour, and Old Sorrel lifted her head and looked out toward the river. A sliver of moon sparkled on the surface, but there wasn't enough light to see by. I could just barely make out the outline of a rowboat about twenty yards from shore. It was so quiet—no sound at all reached my ears though I could see the oars dipping into the water. To my eyes it appeared that only a rower was in that boat, and I was expecting three fugitives.

I got down from the wagon seat and scrambled down the bank to meet the boat. Just as it reached the shore, three heads popped up from the boat's bottom. Apparently the fugitives had been hiding on the bottom of the small boat—two boys and a man. They looked tired and dirty. Without a word, I motioned them to the wagon up on the bank, and wearily they began to move toward it. I turned back to the rower and reached out a hand in silent greeting. He grasped my hand and when I looked at his face, I recognized Mr. Driscol's slave, Sam!

Not a word passed between us, but Sam nodded at me and I knew he remembered me from the lumberyard. Though I'd introduced myself as a Rankin, he'd not said a word about us both being Underground Railroad conductors. I guess we all had our own secrets to keep.

Not long after this event Sam and all of Mr. Driscol's slaves, except for one arthritic old man, ran away. Within a week, the old man also made his escape. Mr. Driscol followed them all the way to Cleveland and reached the wharf just in time to see his "property" climb the schooner's side and, before he could get a legal order to seize them, sail away. Mr. Driscoll believed that we Rankins had something to do with the loss of his slaves. Soon, another reward of $3000 was offered for Father, dead or alive.

> *All through the week men were seen prowling about our premises at night, but as father had positively forbidden them to be molested unless seen to commit some act of depredation, we only kept watch on their movements.* (Lowry's Memoir)

*From my childhood I had a taste for mechanics and de-
lighted in the use of tools and was accustomed to spend
my hours of play in building little boats to sail in the
river, wagons, sleds, etc. I was once sent on an errand
to a woolen mill, which was driven by a horse walking
up an inclined wheel. I took in the design and built just
such a wheel in my father's yard to be run by a favorite
cat, but puss did not relish the tread wheel and vigor-
ously resisted all my efforts to persuade him to travel
on it.* (Lowry's Memoir)

# Chapter 5:
# Lowry's Choice

When I was 14, my father enrolled
me in Ripley College. For a time,
Father was president of that school, so
it was important to him that I go there.
My parents were great believers in the
importance of education. During my
second year at Ripley, Ben Templeton,
a free Black about my age, came to
board with my family on Liberty Hill.
My father struck a bargain with the Presbyterian Church lead-
ers at Chillicothe. He proposed that the Church take on part of
the tuition expenses for Ben so that he could be educated at
Ripley College. The church agreed on the one condition that
Ben would study for the ministry. My parents agreed to pro-
vide room and board for Ben, who was glad for the opportunity
to study at Ripley College and overjoyed at the idea of preparing for the ministry. We attended Ripley College together and
were great friends.

It was also my parents' wish that I study for the ministry, but
by the time I was 16, I felt that I was cut out for an entirely dif-

ferent profession. Ever since I was a young boy, I'd had a fascination with all things mechanical, and in particular, boats. A good many steamers were built in Ripley at that time, and as a youngster I delighted in watching the boat builders as they crafted everything by hand—from the flooring to the most delicate of molding.

"I want to leave Ripley College and apprentice myself as a carpenter," I told my father one day as we were looking at the drawings for enlarging the church. I was in the middle of my senior year at Ripley College and not yet seventeen. My father looked stunned.

"But it has been my—and your mother's—cherished desire that you follow me into the ministry," he said.

"But I do not feel the call for the ministry, Father. You preach that each man must follow God's wishes, not man's, and I do not believe God is calling me to the ministry," I replied. I was trying to be reasonable. One did not win many arguments with Father.

"Then perhaps medicine, some other profession," he suggested.

"I feel it is *my duty* to enter a mechanical career. I wish to become a carpenter," I declared.

What could he say to that—I had used his own words against him. He told me he would have to discuss my wishes with my mother. The next day, they asked to speak with me.

"Although we are greatly disappointed that you do not wish to enter the ministry, we will not insist that you do so if you do not feel the call," said Father. My mother, however, was not yet resigned to my choice.

"Perhaps mission work would interest you. In missions you could combine the work of the ministry with your mechanical interests," she suggested reasonably.

"I wish to learn carpentry. Even if I should graduate with my class at Ripley, I would still be too young to enter the ministry—or any other profession," I insisted. "I want to learn the trade *now.*"

"What God chooses for us is not always what we may choose for ourselves," said Mother.

"Nor what our parents might choose for us," I replied. Sometimes I hated being a Presbyterian.

Even Ben tried to dissuade me from leaving Ripley College. The studious and articulate Ben was a far better student than I was, and truly a scholar. Like my father, he was good with words.

"You are throwing away a great opportunity," said Ben. "A liberal education gives you many tools for changing people and correcting evils."

"The only tools I'm interested in are chisels and saws. I can change plenty with the tools of the carpentry trade," I persisted.

In the end, my parents relented, on two conditions. First, I must promise to return to Ripley College and finish my senior year after my carpenter's apprenticeship was done. Second, I must apprentice with my uncle, William McNish, an architect and carpenter, and the husband of my mother's sister, Lucretia.

That very afternoon, I went to speak with my Uncle Will, who was delighted that I wanted to join him as an apprentice. Aunt Lucretia and Uncle Will lived on Front Street in Ripley, in a large house just a few yards from the Ohio River.

"As apprentice, you'll have to do whatever work needs to be done, nephew or not," warned Uncle Will. "And in exchange for your room and board, you'll be required to help your Aunt around the house whenever she needs it."

I would have done anything to learn my uncle's trade, and his proposal seemed fair enough to me. We agreed that my apprenticeship would last for two years and expire on my nineteenth birthday.

"You will also be required to keep the shop clean and the tools in order. And in the evenings and on Saturdays, you must promise to apply yourself to the study of architecture," said my uncle.

I promised to do whatever was required, and on Monday morning I moved my few belongings and myself from the house on Liberty Hill down to my Aunt and Uncle's house on Front Street. It was the spring of 1833. My sisters Isabella, Julia and Mary and my brothers David, Calvin, Sam, John, Andrew, baby William, and my friend Ben Templeton would carry on the farm work and the Underground Railroad work at Liberty Hill while I applied myself to the skills of carpentry and architecture. I felt as though it was the start of a new life in a whole new world, though I had moved less than a mile from Liberty Hill.

I loved living and working in the town. In 1833 there was not an Ohio town along the river except Cincinnati that was as industrious as Ripley. Hundreds of boats were made in Ripley every year, and in the last five years Ripley had become a major manufacturer of steamboats. My room in my Aunt and Uncle's house faced the riverfront, which was bustling with activity day and night.    Nearby, flatboats called "broad horses" were loaded with thousands of barrels of pork and then floated down the Ohio and Mississippi Rivers into the Southern ports. Only pork was packed because the South did not feed beef to its slaves, Uncle Will explained. The town of Ripley contained several churches, including my father's Presbyterian church that I continued to attend each Sunday. Several mills, stores and a newspaper printing office also operated in the town of Ripley.

The first days of my apprenticeship I was employed on building or refurbishing the cabin of the steamer, *Fair Play*. I delighted in working with the wood, shaping it with the tools my uncle patiently taught me to use, thrilling to the shapes and textures I could create, and to the colors of the wood that I uncovered in the finish work. I learned to carve the intricate molding and to finish the planes of floorboards so that they were as smooth and shiny as a mirror.

In the evenings and on Saturday mornings, I studied architecture at a desk in my room. The windows of my upstairs corner bedroom overlooked Front Street and the Ohio River, with the Kentucky cedared hills beyond—on a clear day I could see all the way to the little village of Charleston, Kentucky. Below my windows, the Ohio River stretched away southwest in full view for two miles or more, ending at the large town of Augusta, Kentucky.

Last spring the great Ohio River had flooded, and most of the houses on Front Street had been filled with water. Though my uncle's house had been spared water on the main living floors, the cellar had flooded. At the time, Uncle Will's father was staying with them, and the old gentleman had come downstairs in the night and by mistake took a door to the cellar instead of the one to the yard. He fell headlong into the cellar full of water and would have drowned had Uncle Will not heard him and come to his rescue. The river was fickle and she could be dangerous, but I loved her, and I thrilled to living in my uncle's house where I could gaze out at the river from almost every window.

My apprenticeship with Uncle Will was going well—I was especially happy when I could ply my new trade on one of the steamers. One afternoon, as I was finishing up my daily work on the *Fair Play*, I was surprised to find my friend Ben Templeton waiting for me at the dock. He was very upset.

"I'm not wanting to bother your parents with this matter, but I can no longer impose upon the kindness of Professor Simpson," he began.

"If it's tutoring you need, you've come to the wrong person," I replied. I had never been able to keep up with Ben academically.

"My grades are fine, Lowry," he said, and I saw that he was amused that I should think he needed tutoring from the likes of me. He grew serious. "It's just that Frank Shaw has sent a letter to the College asking for my dismissal. Shaw says that because his own brother is too poor to go to college, then a "nigra" like me should not be allowed to go either."

Frank Shaw was a known troublemaker and a drunk. His father owned the distillery a few miles outside of Ripley, and his brother Chancy made a living as a slave catcher. There was no love lost between the Rankins and the Shaws, I can tell you.

"Professor Simpson has been escorting me to and from my classes every day because Shaw says that if I am not dismissed, he will cowhide me to within an inch of my life," said Ben. "It is causing no end of embarrassment for me, and I fear it is a great inconvenience to Professor Simpson."

"Then tell Professor Simpson that he no longer needs to trouble himself on your account. If Calvin or David will escort you to the College each morning, I will escort you home at night. Shaw is too much of a coward to try and take on more than one man." At that Ben seemed relieved.

For the next two weeks, I met Ben at Ripley College after his last class. Together, we rode through the Ripley streets in my Uncle's wagon, and on up the steep incline to the house on Liberty Hill. Not once did Frank Shaw approach us, not even the one day we saw him drive his own wagon right past us. He nodded to me as we passed, but said nothing. The next day, Ben said that he felt it would be safe to go to and from school alone.

"He was probably all liquored up when he wrote that letter, and he doesn't even remember it," I said. But the very next day, Frank Shaw met Ben in the street and beat him with a cowhide whip until some of the townspeople put a stop to it. Frank Shaw was arrested and sent to jail, but that was not to be the end of it.

"The beating stirred up a great deal of controversy about whether colored students should be allowed at Ripley College. The Southern students have put pressure on the trustees to dismiss Ben because he is Black," said my father when he came to visit me at Uncle Will's shop a few days later.

"But surely Ben is one of the best students at the College. The trustees will never vote to dismiss him!" I declared.

"In fact it seems that a majority of the trustees favor his dismissal," said my father. "If the trustees vote to dismiss Ben, then no colored person will ever again be allowed to enroll at Ripley College."

"But what of Ben? He's a good student and a good man, and he has his heart set on being a minister. And he has the support of the Church sponsors," I added. My father looked tired. There were so many demands on his time and his conscience. "Ben's sponsors are also the benefactors of Ripley College. If Ben is dismissed, I fear that the school will lose much of its financial support. If he stays, he will always be in danger from those who would harm him because he is Black," he said.

"Seems to me that either way the vote goes will be bad for Ben and bad for the College," I said.

"Then we must ask God to show us a way to keep it from coming to a vote," said Father. He said that a lot. To my way of thinking, the situation needed action, not words.

The next day, Ben voluntarily withdrew from Ripley College. Father offered to teach Ben at home, for it was agreed that at the conclusion of his instruction, Ben would apply for admission to Lane Theological Seminary. Father had good connections there, and he was convinced that Ben Templeton had a call from God to be a minister.

I brooded on the unfairness of it all. I, after all, had made a *choice* not to study at Ripley College. Ben, on the other hand, a much more apt student than I had ever been or could be, was being denied the opportunity just because he was black. But Father had found a way for Ben to continue his studies, and so I was glad for Ben. In the meantime, I felt it was my duty to continue on with my internship.

# Chapter 6:
## Eliza's Escape

One February night during the first winter that I boarded in the house on Front Street, I was at my desk working on an architectural drawing, an assignment from Uncle Will. The chill air made me stiff as I bent over my drawing, but I was determined to present it to my Uncle in the morning. Outside, the wind rattled the tree branches and sleet hit the windowpanes. A thin coat of snow covered the street like a fresh coat of paint. A man walked along Front Street, hunched against the wind and cold. I recognized him as Chancy Shaw, the slave catcher who lived in Ripley. He often patrolled the riverbank at night, hoping to capture some poor escaping slave that he could return to Kentucky for a bounty. He passed beneath my window and I watched him until he was out of sight.

I got up and stretched and stood at the window awhile, watching the ice floes in the river. Something else was moving on the river—not a boat surely, for the partially frozen river was treacherous for any boat, especially in the dark. I leaned forward for a closer look. My breath made a fog on the windowpane, and I wiped it away with my sleeve.

As the object on the river moved closer, I could see that it was a person, leaping from ice cake to ice cake—the figure of woman! And she looked to be carrying a bundle of clothing in her arms. Once or twice she stumbled and fell to her knees, still holding tightly to her bundle, and I felt sure she would slip into the frigid river between the ice cakes and drown.

I ran out of the house and to the riverbank. The woman was still struggling across the precarious bridge of ice, and as she got closer I saw that her bundle was really a small child wrapped in a shawl! Finally, she made it to the riverbank, and just as she stepped onto the riverbank, a figure stepped out of the shadows and gave her a hand. It was Chancy Shaw! I ran forward, not knowing how I would rescue the woman from Chancy, and not caring. I only knew I must help her.

"Let her go!" I shouted. The woman slumped to the ground still clutching her child who had begun to wail. Chancy turned to face me then, and I was sure there would be a struggle.

"Anyone crossing that river carrying a baby has earned her freedom," said Chancy. Then he disappeared up the alley.

I turned back to the woman. She was shaking violently and her skirt was stiff with ice. I took the crying child from her. The shawl wrapped around him was soaked with the muddy, icy river water, so I tossed the shawl on the riverbank and wrapped him in my own coat.

"Please hide me. My chile's bein' sold," the woman whispered. Her teeth chattered. I helped her up the riverbank. We reached the road a few feet away and the woman stopped and looked up. I followed her eyes. From any point on the river front, except where the buildings were so close together as to block the view, I could see our house on Liberty Hill with its light burning in the window—the one my Mother lit every night as a beacon to any runaway who might seek shelter there.

"I want to go there," she said. "They'se good people there who will help me n' my chile," she whispered. There was no time to waste. I would have to get this woman and her child to shelter or they would surely perish in the cold.

She said her name was Eliza and she was running away to join her husband in Canada. I thought it best to take the fugitives to Liberty Hill without delay. If the river ice was breaking up, the ferry would be in operation by daylight—with slave hunters on it. I carried Eliza's child as we climbed the steep stairs that led up the hill to my parents' house.

My mother greeted us and hurried about gathering dry clothes and food Eliza and her child, a boy who looked to be about two years old. His name was Harry. My father served them hot tea.

"My husband run away six months ago, and I promised I'd follow when I had our little one ready to run with us. But then the mistress, she got word of my plan and tol' me she gonna sell this little one tomorrow, so's I up and run today. Had to leave the older chillun behind," said Eliza.

"You and Harry are safe now. We'll see that you never have to go back," Mother assured Eliza as she gathered up the wet, muddy clothes.

"Oh no, ma'am. I be coming back alright. Soon as it gets warm, I be crossing dat ole river agin to get my other chillun— I gots five more of 'em," said Eliza.

I thought her very brave for saying it, but we all knew that Eliza, or anyone who attempted to entice Eliza's other children to run off, would be facing a great risk. The children would be watched closely now that both parents had escaped. Eliza faced the likelihood of getting caught and hung if she returned to retrieve her children—or worse, they could all be torn apart by the dogs. Anyone caught helping them to escape in Kentucky faced a long stay in prison.

We sat with Eliza in front of the fire while she and Harry drank tea and ate my Mother's good, thick wheat bread slathered in rich butter. We debated whether the fugitives should move on right away or if they could afford to stay the night for the warmth and rest they needed so badly.

"The ferry won't run until daybreak. They can get a few hours rest here, surely," said Mother, as she gathered blankets to make up beds for Eliza and Harry.

"But if Eliza's mistress is so desperate to keep her, slave hunters will find a way to cross that river tonight," said Father. "I think it's best for them to move on to Red Oak tonight."

"The babe is chilled through. He needs to sleep. It's best for both of them to get some rest—it'll be a hard journey tomorrow," Mother protested.

Father finally agreed. It was two in the morning when I left the house on Liberty Hill and returned to my Aunt and Uncle's house on Front Street.

The next morning, three Kentucky men rode into Ripley and started asking around about a runaway woman and child. I knew it wouldn't be long before they'd be heading straight up to Liberty Hill. I wondered if the brave and determined Eliza was still there, or if my brothers had taken her on to the next depot already.

I thought about the beacon of light my mother left burning in the window as a sign to any runaway seeking shelter there. Why couldn't I set a similar beacon from my Aunt and Uncle's house on Front Street—a signal to Liberty Hill that slave hunters were in town? Such a light would signal my parents that any fugitives on Liberty Hill should be hurried on their way.

My uncle's third floor attic vent faced Liberty Hill. If I could build some steps to reach the high vent in the roof, I could place a lantern there as a signal whenever slave hunters were in the area. I would speak to my Uncle about my plan right away.

*On entering my room I sat down at the drafting board. I had on it an unfinished draft of a stairway that was to be erected in a given imaginary space where it would be very difficult to build one easy of ascent.* (Lowry's Memoir)

# Chapter 7:
# Rev. Rankin's Disguise

In a few days, I had designed and built a set of wooden steps—eight in all—that led from my Uncle's attic floor to the roof vent. I mounted an iron hook to the rafter and hung a lantern from it. Then I climbed the hill to tell my parents about this new signal.

"A lantern light from Uncle's roof means that slave hunters have been spotted in town," I said.

"And if you should see that a lantern fails to burn in the window on Liberty Hill, that is a signal that it is not safe for a fugitive slave to come to us," said Father.

During that spring I worked hard to learn the skills of carpentry and architecture. I also kept my eyes and ears alert for news of escaping slaves. I watched for the faces of strangers. I listened for news about slave hunters in Ripley. Sometimes when the air was very still, sounds from the Kentucky side of the river drifted across the river. Twice when the weather was fine and I had my windows open, I had been awakened to the sound of bloodhounds baying at the scent of their prey. Both times, I lit the lantern in the attic.

One Sunday afternoon, I was visiting my family on Liberty Hill. Mother had sent me to the garden to harvest the first of the peas. It was a bright day in mid June, and there was muggi-

ness in the air that meant we'd have a thunderstorm before
dark. I was bent over the row of peas when I caught some
movement in the blackberry bushes near the barn. I straight-
ened up and was startled to see a young Black boy crouching
behind the bushes. He was signaling to me.

"I come back for my babies," whispered the boy when I got
near. He would not leave the shelter of the bushes that were in
the deep shadow of our barn.

"Inside. Quickly," I whispered and opened the heavy barn
doors. I smelled the sweet hay. Dust curled in the rays of
sunlight that filtered through the barn boards.

"Lowry, it's me," said the boy, and I was startled that he
knew my name, for I had been sure he was a fugitive slave
seeking shelter on Liberty Hill. The boy took off his hat.

"Eliza!"

"Said I'd be back come fair weather. I'se goin' to Kentucky
to fetch my chillun," said Eliza. Her shoulders were slumped in
exhaustion, but there was a determined set to her jaw that told
me there was no stopping her at what she'd set her mind on. "I
left the babe with George, and now I come back to get the others jes like I says I would."

I hid Eliza in the secret barn cellar and went to the house to
tell my parents. Within the hour, I was sent down the hill into
the village to arrange passage for Eliza to Kentucky. I was able
to rent a skiff large enough for six people, and after paying the
owner, I rowed it to a secluded place and hid it on the riverbank.

Although it was unlikely that Eliza's former owner would
still be looking for her after she had been gone almost five
months, we thought it safest for her to cross the river in the
middle of the night, fetch her children, and recross the river
under cover of darkness. For the rest of the day, I watched the
river for any signs of slave hunters, but Ripley had been pretty
quiet lately.

At midnight, I went to the skiff to wait for Eliza. Twenty
minutes later, my bother David came down the road with the

wagon hitched to Old Sorrel. I knew Eliza was hidden under the false bottom of the wagon bed, and I pushed the hay aside, and helped her out. Eliza now wore a gown and a headscarf.

"Hurry, Eliza. And you'd best be back before daybreak. Bring nothing but the children—bundles will only slow you down," I warned her as I helped her into the skiff I'd borrowed and handed her the oars. Lightening was flashing to the west, and I could hear thunder rumble in the distance. A storm could be good. Everyone would likely be inside when Eliza arrived at the plantation, and the noise of the storm might mask the sounds of their escape. I gave the skiff a shove off shore and watched Eliza row slowly across the dark Ohio.

All night I sat by my open window listening for a sign that Eliza and her five children had made a safe escape. The thunder and lightening increased and then moved off to the south. The storm had missed Ripley, but a cool blanket of air descended on the Ohio valley and a wall of fog began to move down the river. Then I could see nothing. I closed my eyes and listened, and once I thought I heard baying hounds in the distance. The sky turned from black to gray, but there was no sign of Eliza and her children.

At noon, I was surprised by a visit from my father. My aunt brought him to the wood shop where I was helping my uncle to rout some molding.

"Just came to say hi to my boy," said Father to Uncle Will who seemed pleased about the unexpected visitor. Uncle Will was an abolitionist, but he was no Underground Railroader, believing it in the best interest of his own family to abide by the law. My uncle knew nothing of Eliza, for we Rankins knew better than to speak of our activities except to each other. It was safest for everyone that way.

"Did the lantern burn out last night?" Father asked. I knew this to mean that he wanted to know if I'd heard any news of Eliza and her children.

"Didn't need one last night," I replied. Father went home. Everything stayed quiet in Ripley all afternoon, but the fog hung over the river so dense that I couldn't see or hear a thing that might be happening on the Kentucky shore. It was almost suppertime when the fog lifted. From my upstairs window, I counted thirty-one men or horseback, with dogs and guns, patrolling the Kentucky shore. With apologies to my aunt who was just setting the table for our evening meal, I left the house and raced up the hill to tell my parents. No lantern was necessary, for Eliza and her children apparently had not made it across the Ohio.

"We'll pray that Eliza and the children have a safe haven at Abe's," said Father. Abe Courtney was my father's friend, an anti-slavery man who lived in Maysville, Kentucky. "I told her to go there if she was chased and to wait there until she could get to the skiff safely," said Father.

"But Eliza and the children can't get to the skiff at all if the slave hunters are patrolling the shore," I said after I told him what I'd seen on the Kentucky side.

Mother had a plan. She rushed from the room and came back holding out one of her dresses and a headscarf.

"You must take the ferry across the river. Once there, put these clothes on and give chase to the slave hunters so that Eliza and her children have time to get to the skiff," said Mother, and to my amazement, when she held out the dress to my father, he took it without a moment's hesitation.

"But Mother, surely you don't want Father to actually cross the river! If he gets caught, the penalty is 21 years in prison." It was one thing to help a fugitive from slavery once he or she was on the Ohio side of the river, but the stakes were high in Kentucky for those who helped them get away. And there was a bounty on my father's life.

I looked at the faces of my family—what would become of Mother and the younger children if Father was caught? As an apprentice, I had no salary at all, and although my father's salary as a preacher was small, our large family could not live without it. But Mother stood firm.

"Please Father, don't do this," I begged, thinking about the price on my father's head, dead or alive. If caught, and his identity were discovered, the scoundrel slave hunters might very well kill Father for the bounty.

"I will go because it is the right thing to do," said Father. But I didn't see it that way. Not then. I saw the plan as a selfish act of a man who would sacrifice his family to help strangers, and I didn't think it was very admirable at all.

"Eliza is counting on us to help her and her children," said Mother. "You do what you think is best, Lowry."

"We'll put this in God's hands," said Father, as he took the clothing from my mother and called for David to saddle Old Sorrel.

"I'll saddle Old Sorrel—and Fly," I said. As much as I hated the whole idea, I couldn't let Father go across the river alone.

# Chapter 8:
# On the Kentucky Side
# of the River

The ferryman pulled on the rope that moved the boat across the Ohio River's strong current.

"Hope you 'n yer boy ain't plannin' on getting back tonight, Rev. Rankin," said the ferryman as he hauled on the rope. "This trip's my last for today."

"Won't be returning until tomorrow, thanks. Thought we'd come over tonight and stay in Maysville so as to get an early start in the morning. We've got business downstate," said Father. He did not lie, except that it was "downstate Ohio," not Kentucky, where the business would take place once we got back to Ripley and arranged for Eliza and her family to travel to Canada.

The ferryman grunted in reply. He was a pro-slavery man himself and didn't think much of the abolitionists. He knew Rev. Rankin to be one of them.

As we approached the Kentucky shore, we saw the slave hunters still patrolling the waterfront in the dusk. We could no longer hear the hounds, but Eliza had baffled the hounds once before, and I knew she could do it again with so much at stake. I was hopeful that she and her family were safe at Abe Courtney's.

By the time we gathered the horses and led them up the ramp from the ferry wharf, it was dark and the edges of the shore were lined with ghostly silver. I looked up and saw a sliver of moon emerge from behind the clouds. Father and I rode a few yards down the road to a wooded area, where we dismounted. Father changed into his disguise. If there hadn't been so much at stake, the sight of my father in a dress would have been hilarious.

"I'll ride Fly down the road and then tie him in the woods, while I show myself to the slave hunters. Then I'll retrieve Fly and head back here to get my clothes," said Father. My job was to take Old Sorrel and retrieve Eliza and her children from the Courtney house as quickly as possible, then accompany them in the skiff across the river to Ripley.

"I'll take Eliza and the children to Liberty Hill, and meet you at the ferry on this side tomorrow at noon," I said. I embraced him, and as I did so I wondered if this would be the last time for many years, maybe ever, that I would see him. Then I watched him ride off and I prayed that he would be safe.

I urged Old Sorrel on down the road until we reached the village of Maysville. We slowed down so as not to attract attention. Several times, I thought I heard gunfire, and once I know I heard the hounds. Soon, I found the Courtney house and rapped on the door. Mrs. Courtney recognized me at once. She let me in and led me to the kitchen. There, she pulled back a woven rug, and I helped her lift the heavy door set flush into the wooden floor. Mrs.Courtney handed me a lantern, and I lifted it high so that its light shone into the cellar hole.

There sat Eliza on the dirt floor amongst the turnips and the onions, her five children huddled around her. Two of the children were teenagers, one of them a girl who looked about my age. The younger children ranged between the ages of ten and three, I guessed, and they looked frightened and confused, as though they were about to die. Maybe they were. Not one of them had shoes. Eliza squinted up at where I stood silhouetted in the light. She looked fearful and uncertain—exactly the way I felt.

"It's Lowry, come to take you to Liberty Hill," I said as I descended into the dark cellar. Eliza grinned.

"Praise be! I freed my babies—every one of 'em!" Indeed she had. I have never known a braver woman—or man either, for that matter, except for my father.

It was full dark when we left the Courtney house. The clouds had covered the sliver of new moon. Eliza and her oldest girl, Jane, helped the younger children climb down the slippery riverbank while I hauled the skiff out of its hiding place and dragged it to the river. I could smell its pungent, fishy odor, and I saw river debris floating along the shore. I wondered if we would be able to find our way across the river in the pitch dark. Everything was quiet, until the youngest child began to whimper.

"Shush," said Jane as she pulled the child onto her lap in the crowded skiff. The word had no sooner left her mouth when three figures slipped out of the gloom and came toward us on the shore.

"Get in! Quick! They comin'" Eliza ordered her children. In a panic they piled into the skiff, nearly capsizing it. I pushed off from the shore and quickly rowed out into the current. I heard a gunshot and realized one of the men was shooting at us. But the blackness that I had worried about just a moment before now swallowed the shore behind us. I pulled at the oars for what seemed like an hour, and then I heard the welcome sound of water lapping the Ohio shore. We had made it to free soil at last.

I left Eliza and her family on the riverbank. From there Eliza would take them to Liberty Hill. She knew the way. I wished I could go with them and climb into bed and sleep for a week, but there was no time to waste. I ran to my Uncle's house to light the lantern in the attic, for there was no way to know whether or not the men who spotted us on the shore would find a way across the river tonight or wait until the ferry was running in the morning. Then I had to get back to Kentucky before daylight so that I could fetch Old Sorrel at the Courtneys and meet my father at the ferry by noon. As I pushed the skiff off from shore the second time that night, I wondered if Father would be there to meet me the next day. Or was he even now in jail—or perhaps worse?

*. . . an anti-slavery society was formed of one hundred members. I was one of that hundred.* (Lowry's Memoir)

# Chapter 9:
# A Visit
# From Harriett Beecher

Two hours hour later I was at the Courtney place. I went directly to the barn to check on Old Sorrel. I had ridden her pretty hard that night, and I wanted to make sure she was OK. When I entered the barn, the sweet smell of hay and leather and horseflesh greeted me. I went to the closest stall and checked on Old Sorrel. To my great relief, I saw that Fly was right beside her in the next stall. So Father had made his escape too!

Father and I and the horses took the noon ferry back across the Ohio River. Somehow, we had managed to escape suspicion for now. At Liberty Hill, Mother told us that Eliza and her family were already headed north. They had been sent on within an hour of their arrival at Liberty Hill.

"I saw your beacon from the roof, Lowry, and I knew that it would not be safe to keep them here," she said.

Eliza and her children had left the house hidden under a wagonload of bran, and we later heard that they made it safely to Canada to be reunited with George and Harry—an entire family had escaped their hateful bondage.

I returned to my Aunt and Uncle 's house on Front Street and applied myself to my apprenticeship. During the week I worked as a carpenter building boats, and I continued to study architecture with Uncle Will. Most of all, I loved building the steamers and being close to the river. The river was always moving, and I felt the river current flowed through my life as blood in my veins. I thought that I would be forever happy if I could always find work on the river.

On Sundays I attended the service at my father's Presbyterian Church and then stayed for the anti-slavery lectures that were delivered by a number of visiting speakers. At the time of my apprenticeship, my father's church was filled with people who came to hear the Sunday anti-slavery lectures, and afterwards the house on Liberty Hill seemed always filled with visitors. It was after one of those lectures, which I always attended when I could, that I met Harriett Beecher and her father, Lyman Beecher, the famous preacher and president of the faculty of Lane Theological Seminary in nearby Cincinnati. With them was Rev. Calvin Stowe, who was to marry Harriett.

One evening at the end of my Sunday visit to Liberty Hill, I sat on the porch with Harriett, discussing the morning's anti-slavery lecture.

"I've hated slavery since I was a little girl," said Harriet.

"But you grew up in New England—so far from the slave states. How could you acquire such a hatred of something you had never seen?" I asked.

"Aunt Mary's husband was a planter, and he owned many slaves. Aunt Mary told us of his cruelties. If I live to be a hundred, I will never forget the stories she told," said Harriett. Her Aunt Mary had finally run away from her husband and come to live with the Beechers when Harriet was a child, she said.

"Then you are as eager as I am to see the slaves in this country set free," I said.

"Oh indeed!" she replied. "Though perhaps not in the same way that you Rankins think. I believe that a sudden emancipation would disrupt this country so that it would never recover. It might even start a civil war," said Harriet.

Until then I had thought that all those who hated slavery wished for the complete and sudden emancipation of the slaves.

"How do you believe slavery should be ended, then?"

"I favor the colonization idea, which would free the slaves gradually, educate them so that they may prosper, and then send them to Africa to establish a colony there," said Harriett. But I disagreed. Any institution as awful as slavery ought to be ended right then and there, I thought.

Although Harriett and I did not agree entirely on the emancipation issue, I discovered that she shared my strong convictions about helping fugitives.

"Once when I was in Washington, Kentucky, I saw a slave auctioned off in the town square. The poor fellow's hands and feet were chained together, but he stood tall and looked his buyer straight in the eye. I shall never forget his face or the dignity which he kept even as he was led away by his new owner," said Harriett.

Then I told her about the courageous slave, Eliza, and how she had escaped with her little boy and run across the ice, risking both their lives. I was very careful not to mention my role in Eliza's escape, for secrecy was the rule for those of us in the Underground Railroad.

"My father and brothers and Rev. Stowe all preach against slavery, just as your father does. We've seen the power of words to make changes in how people *think*, but if we are to end slavery we must use words that change the way people *feel*," she said.

"Perhaps you can preach on paper as your father and brothers use their voices," I suggested. I knew her to be a published author as the previous summer Harriett had co- written a geography book with her older sister Catherine. I told Harriett something of the power of my father's early writings and the letters he had written to his brother, Thomas Rankin, who once owned slaves in Virginia.

"Uncle Thomas finally brought his slaves to Ohio and set them free. He provided them with homes and money so that they could get a good start and they have prospered," I said.

"Perhaps one day I shall write something that will make this whole nation feel what an accursed thing slavery is," she said.

"But what of you, Lowry? If you care so deeply about ending slavery, why are you not preparing to enter the ministry where you might reach those in most need of hearing these ideas? I know it was your parents' wish," said Harriet.

It was true that I had helped hundreds of runaway slaves to freedom—I had acted with the courage of my conviction, surely. But, I reflected, I had really done nothing to stop slavery—to end it once and for all.

"I am not a man of words," I said thinking of my apprenticeship. "though I do what I can to assist the anti-slavery cause."

"Ah Lowry, you are yet young. A man cannot ravel out the stitches in which early days have knit him," she said. I couldn't know it then, but I know now that Harriett had prophesized two events that evening that would change the course of my life and of countless others.

*An event occurred one day in the middle of December 1834 that changed all my plans and revolutionized the whole purpose of my life. . . . A rumor reached us that there was being built in Pittsburgh, for the Cincinnati and New Orleans trade, a steamer twice as large as any boat then on the Ohio and Mississippi rivers. Everyone was anxious to see the big steamboat, which was named* Uncle Sam. (Lowry's Memoir)

# *Chapter 10: Lowry's Vow*

I worked all the summer and fall of 1834 on the cabin of the steamer *Fair Play*. It was delicate, painstaking work that I enjoyed. The fragrance of the wood drifted through the cabin as I sanded the floorboards until they were smooth as glass. The wood was still warm from the friction of the sanding when I smoothed my hand over the surface, feeling for rough spots. The wood was like a living thing beneath my palm. How I loved this work, especially because it brought me near the water.

My Uncle Will worked beside me, supervising me when necessary, but by now I had learned most of the skills of the trade. We talked amiably as we worked. I have always had a great affection for my Uncle.

"I hear the new steamer *Uncle Sam* is tied up at the town wharf," I said.

He too had heard that report and was most anxious to visit the *Uncle Sam* and examine her construction.

"They say she's the biggest boat on the river, twice as big as the *Fair Play*," I said. Uncle Will and I resolved to visit her first thing in the morning.

We visited her cabin first, so that we could compare her craftsmanship with that of our own. When I was satisfied that my own work on the Fair Play was comparable, I wandered around the lower deck for a while before visiting the engine room. I'd heard that the *Uncle Sam* was a fully loaded cargo steamer, but I was unprepared for the sight that met my eyes when I emerged from the engine room. There in front of me were two groups of slaves. A line of half naked men was handcuffed to a chain that was attached to one side of the deck, and the same number of women was handcuffed to a chain on the other side. In all, there were about fifty slaves. There were no chairs or bedding, and it looked as though the slaves had been chained there for a long time. A few were sitting with their backs against the side, but others were lying down as best they could with their handcuffs and chains, which were just barely long enough for them to recline.

At the extreme end of the women's chain was a young woman of not more than twenty. She had long, wavy black hair. She was beautiful on the outside, with her crystal green eyes and light brown skin. But when I looked into those eyes, I saw nothing. No one was there, for how could there be? In order to endure her circumstance, her soul had to have left her body.

I was astounded by the woman's beauty, and I could not fathom that she might be bound for a Southern port to stand on the auction block. And then I was overcome with shame for myself, that I would feel more sympathy for this one young woman than I would for the others just because I thought her beautiful. I might have left the *Uncle Sam* with nothing more than a more intense hatred of slavery had I not overheard the conversation of two men who were approaching the slaves from the other side of the deck.

"This one's special. She'll get the price in Lexington for a fancy girl," said one of the men. He had the look of a slave trader. His hair was long and stringy, and his face was shaded by the kind of broad-brimmed hat worn by so many men in the South. He carried a rawhide cane.

"She's lovely," said his companion. This young man was tall, good-looking, and well dressed. He stopped directly in front of the young woman and looked closely at her. She turned away, and the trader grabbed her roughly by the arm, and shoved her towards the young man as far as her chains allowed. On the other side of the deck, one of the slave men cursed.

"No more of that you black sons of bitches," he growled at the chained men. Then he struck the young woman on the shoulder with his rawhide cane and ordered her to stand still. She obeyed, but her dull lifeless eyes would not meet the eyes of the man who was bargaining for her. I had met plenty of runaways in my life, and to a person they had been brave, reckless, sometimes fearful, but always full of life and hope once they'd reached us. This young woman chained to the ship was nothing but a shell of a person, and all life seemed to have drained out of her. Bondage had done this to her.

"A good mistress she'll make you, this one. She's worth far more than the $2500 I'm asking." The young man offered $2000 for her. The trader shook his head and played his last card.

"Why don't you take her to your room and try her out. It will cost you nothing. Then you'll see that she's worth every dollar of the price I ask." The young man appeared tempted, but he continued to bargain. Clearly, he wanted her. I turned away in disgust.

*As I left the boat my indignation reached the boiling point over the wicked transaction and lifting my right hand toward the heavens, I said aloud, "My God helping me there shall be a perpetual war between me and*

*human slavery in this nation of which I am a member
and I pray God I may never be persuaded to give up the
fight until slavery is dead or the Lord calls me home.*"
(Lowry's Memoir)

My uncle came to stand beside me as I uttered my oath. "Is
that you swearing, Lowry?" he asked.

"I have just seen fifty chained slaves borne like hogs to the
market, and I am angry," I explained. "I have sworn to kill
slavery."

"I guess you'll die long before slavery is killed," was my
Uncle's reply. He did not say this in a mean way, but clearly
Uncle Will did not think that slavery would soon be ended.

I was still angry when I joined my Aunt and Uncle for sup-
per at their house on Front Street. I told my Aunt what I had
witnessed. She shook her head in disgust when I told her about
the slaves chained to the sides of the *Uncle Sam*, but she
agreed with Uncle Will that the slave trade was not likely to
end anytime soon.

"Let not the sun go down on your anger, Lowry," she said
kindly as I left the table, my meal barely touched.

"I guess your advice comes too late in the day for that," I replied.

I climbed the stairs to my darkened room and lit the lamp on
my desk. I had vowed to do all I could to end slavery—now, I
asked myself, what was I going to do about it?

I sat down at my desk. Its surface was cluttered with my architectural drawings. The one on top was the finished draft of
the stairway I had built in the attic, from floor to roof. Eight
steps. Those stairs were the finest thing I ever made with my
own hands, then or since. I lifted my gaze to the window. In
the darkness, my beloved Ohio River sparkled in the ghostly
December moonlight as the current rippled the muddy waters.
It just ran on and on with a life of its own. I thought of Eliza
and the countless other fugitives who had crossed those waters
in their quest for freedom—never able to stop moving until

they reached Canada where they could be truly free. But how sweet was that freedom if they had to leave loved ones behind forever and could not choose where they wished to live?

I loved the river. Its waters always kept moving. A stairway was different. It had a beginning and an end, as did the attic stairway I had built from my own design. Today, I had vowed to end slavery so that no one would ever have need to climb that attic stairway again. I thought, too, about the long stairway I had built with my brothers, with its stone steps leading up to the house on Liberty Hill. Today, I had vowed to end slavery so that no fugitive slave would ever need to climb those steps again. But then it occurred to me that slavery made slaves of us all. The slave owners were slaves to their sin. Those of us in the Underground Railroad were slaves to our obligation to help fugitives. Slave, owner, and conductor—every one of us was a slave to fear.

I remembered Harriet Beecher's words, that "A man cannot ravel out the stitches in which early days have knit him." Perhaps my destiny was, after all, like my father's— to change the world through words, not through carpentry. Is that what Harriett had meant? After all, I had been wrong about my father—he had shown that he could be a man of action AND words. Maybe I could be both too.

Although I didn't relish going back to my studies, much preferring to work with my hands, the point was not to *become* a preacher, but to *be* one. In that way I could spread the idea of emancipation to many people in many places. After pacing the floor of my room all night, I made one more vow that night—I would quit the dream of becoming an architect, much as I wanted to be one, and take up the profession of preacher, so that I could spread the word of abolition. And while I studied for the ministry, I would stay with the work of the Underground Railroad so that more fugitives could escape that hateful institution so long as it lasted.

I stayed awake most of the night thinking about this plan. At dawn, I stood at the window watching the swirling current of the Ohio River and then let my gaze wander to the Kentucky hills beyond. How many fugitives were hiding in those hills at that very moment just waiting for the chance to cross the river? How many more slaves must I help to safety before the practice of slavery was ended once and for all? As the sun brightened the hills, I slipped quietly out of my uncle's house and made my way towards Liberty Hill.

# *Afterword*

Adam Lowry Rankin graduated from the Lane Theological Seminary in 1840, became a minister and like his father, preached abolition. While at seminary, Lowry made 300 Underground Railroad trips, helping escaping slaves. Lowry became a member of the secret Fugitive Slave Vigilance Committee and a publishing agent of the Ohio Anti-Slavery Society. He later served as a chaplain in the Civil War. Adam Lowry Rankin died in 1895.

When Harriett Beecher Stowe's brother, the famous preacher Henry Ward Beecher, was once asked who abolished slavery, he answered, "Rev. John Rankin and his sons did it."

Lowry and his family lived to see four million slaves freed, but not in the way they had hoped to have it done. Had the North purchased the slaves and then freed them as the Rankins had wished, thousands of lives would have been saved from bloody death. The prolonged practice of slavery and the onset of Civil War in this country brought untold suffering to millions. Nearly 620,000 soldiers would die in the 4-year Civil War, leaving countless widows and orphans. In the Civil War to come, human misery would transcend race.

# *Illustrations*

**Adam Lowry Rankin**. Ohio Historical Society.
Used with permission.

# OHIO UNDERGROUND
# RAILROAD ROUTES

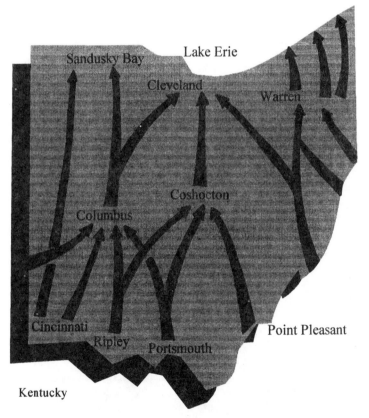

**Map of Ohio's Underground Railroad trails**, showing routes leading north from Ripley in the southwest portion of the state. Information source: Seibert, *The Mysteries of Ohio's Underground Railroads.*

**Ripley as seen from the Kentucky side of the Ohio**, drawn by Henry Howe in 1846. The Rankin house sits high on the bluff overlooking the river.

**Southeast view of the Rankin house** before restoration, 1936. Courtesy of Library of Congress, Historic American Buildings Survey.

**The front of the restored Rankin house today**. When Lowry lived on Liberty Hill, the house included an attached dormitory on one side and a summer kitchen on the other. The outbuildings of Lowry's day are also gone, but the main house structure seen here is maintained by Ripley Heritage, Inc. and is open to the public. Photo by the author.

**The back of the Rankin house today.**
Photo by the author.

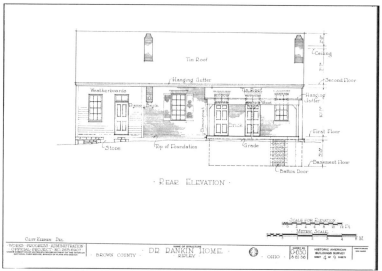

**Engineer's renderings of the Rankin house(1936).** Bottom sketch shows a basement underneath a portion of the building, possibly used to shelter runaway slaves, although such a use has never been documented. Courtesy of Library of Congress, Historic American Buildings Survey.

**View of the town of Ripley, Ohio, and the Ohio River**, taken from the Rankin property. Photo by the author.

**The lantern left in the widow of the front room of the Rankin house on Liberty Hill was a beacon of safety for runaway slaves.** There is some evidence that when the Rankins lived on Liberty Hill, family members may have raised a lantern on a flagpole near the house to signal fugitives to cross the river. Photo by the author.

**Remnants of the stone "freedom stairs" that led from the
town of Ripley up to the Rankin house on Liberty Hill.** The
citizens of Ripley replaced some of the steps with wooden
stairs in 1995. Photo by the author.

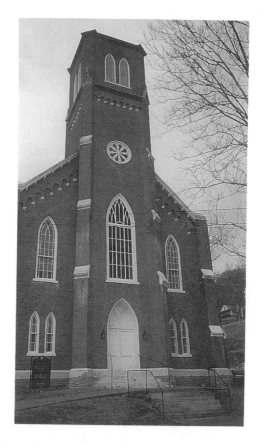

**Rev. Rankin's First Presbyterian Church in Ripley as it looks today.** This is the site where Rev. Rankin first preached when the family moved to Ripley. The original church was built in 1816, then rebuilt in 1834, 1854 and finally, in 1867. Photo by the author.

**Eliza crossing the ice with her child,** as shown in Harriett Beecher Stowe's *Uncle Tom's Cabin.*

**Harriett Beecher Stowe**. Courtesy of Library of Congress.

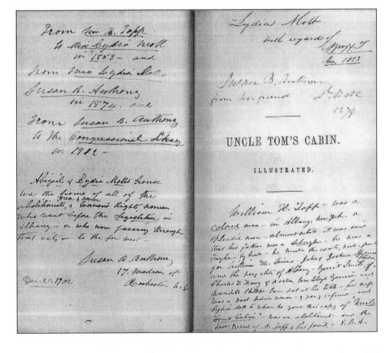

**Copy of *Uncle Tom's Cabin* annotated by women's rights activist Susan B. Anthony,** given to her by abolitionist Lydia Mott. The book by Harriett Beecher Stowe was published in 1852 and sold more than 300,000 copies in its first year. Courtesy of Library of Congress.

**This sketch of a fugitive slave has been a famous anti-slavery symbol since the early 1800s.** Reportedly, a sign bearing this image was once erected on a road leading to Oberlin, Ohio. Oberlin, like Ripley, was notorious for its abolitionist activities before the Civil War. Courtesy of Library of Congress.

**$150 REWARD.**

RANAWAY from the subscriber, on the night of Monday the 11th July, a negro man named

# TOM,

about 30 years of age, 5 feet 6 or 7 inches high; of dark color; heavy in the chest; several of his jaw teeth out; and upon his body are several old marks of the whip, one of them straight down the back. He took with him a quantity of clothing, and several hats.

A reward of $150 will be paid for his apprehension and security, if taken out of the State of Kentucky; $100 if taken in any county bordering on the Ohio river; $50 if taken in any of the interior counties except Fayette; or $20 if taken in the latter county.

july 12-84-tf          **B. L. BOSTON.**

---

**PUBLIC NOTICE.**

THIS day was committed to the custody of the sheriff of Randolph county, State of Illinois, as Runaway, a Negro Man who calls himself

## Martin Barker,

about forty-three years of age, about five feet nine inches high, a scar over his right eye, and also one on his right leg above his ancle, his make and his appearance active; he states that he once belonged to Lewis Barker, of Pope county near the Rock-in-Cave but that he is now free. If any person has any legal claim to him, they are requested to exhibit the same and pay all charges, according to law.

ANT. DUFOUR, *D Sheriff*
For Thos. J. V. Owen, S R C.

*Kaskaskia Dec. 11, 1826*          21-6t

**Fugitive slave posters.** Courtesy of Library of Congress

# *Acknowledgments*

I am grateful for the support of The Research Council of Kent State University, which made possible the research and writing of this book.

Many individuals inspired and encouraged me during the research stage of this project. George Williston first suggested I investigate the Southern Ohio Underground Railroad and its operators. Thanks also to the late Jim Caccamo, historian and scholar, whose interest in the Northeast Ohio's Underground Railroad was an inspiration and foundation for my early research. Sadly, Jim died during the writing of this book.

Others were helpful during the writing stage of the project. I'd like to thank Jacqueline Rowser, Professor of Pan African Studies at Kent State University, for her insightful comments on an early draft of the book as well as on the question-and-answer section. Dr. Rowser leads a popular KSU summer workshop titled "Uncovering the Mysteries of the Underground Railroad." Thanks also to Dr. Leonne Hudson of KSU's History Department for setting me straight on a few things. Any errors in the book are my own.

I am profoundly grateful to Alison Gibson, Director of the Union Township Public Library in Ripley. Alison promptly answered all of my many questions regarding the history of Ripley. It was Alison who first brought Adam Lowry Rankin's Autobiography to my attention.

Thanks to Betty Campbell, President of Ripley Heritage, Inc., who opened up the historic Rankin house during the off-season so that my husband and I could tour the building and grounds. I am also grateful for her comments on an early draft of this story. Betty's knowledge of the Rankin family and the Underground Railroad activity of the early Ripley citizens is unsurpassed.

I'd like to thank Vic and Betsy Billingsley, owners of the Signal House Bed and Breakfast, for the hospitality of their home and library, and for showing me the attic steps that became a part of my story. I am also grateful to John Mattox, Curator of the Underground Railroad Museum in Flushing, Ohio, for sharing his collection with me; and to my friend and fellow writer Jane Ann Turzillo for helping me to ask all the right questions. Thanks to my friend and colleague Dr. Tom Davis for his ongoing encouragement of and unique insight into all my research and writing projects.

Finally, I wish to thank my husband Rollie and my children Scott and Katy for their loving support and patience.

# Student/Teacher Resources

Timeline: Ohio Anti-Slavery Laws and Adam Lowry Rankin's Underground Railroad Activity

| | |
|---|---|
| 1787 | Slavery outlawed in Northwest Territory, which includes Ohio. |
| 1803 | Ohio admitted to Union as a free state. |
| 1804 | Ohio's Black Laws passed, making it illegal to aid escaping slaves or to interfere with their capture. |
| 1807 | $100 is added to the fine of those caught helping runaways. |
| 1816 | Adam Lowry Rankin born to Rev. John and Jean Rankin. |
| 1822 | Rankin family moves to Ripley, Ohio. |
| 1829 | Rankin family moves to house on "Liberty Hill" overlooking the Ohio River. |
| 1832 | Harriet Beecher moves to Cincinnati with her family and visits Ripley the next year. |
| 1833 | Adam Lowry Rankin begins his internship. |
| 1836 | Adam Lowry Rankin enters Lane Theological Seminary, Cincinnati, OH. |
| 1839 | Ohio passes new law that levies $500 fine and a prison term of 60 days to those caught helping fugitive slaves. The law allows any Black to be taken into custody based on a warrant issued by any judge, justice of the peace, or mayor. |
| 1848-9 | Ohio House debates seceding from the Union in protest over continued slavery in the south. |

| | |
|---|---|
| 1851 | Harriet Beecher Stowe begins writing *Uncle Tom's Cabin* which is published the following year. |
| 1861 | Outbreak of Civil War. |
| 1863 | Emancipation Proclamation. |
| 1865 | Civil War ends and slavery abolished once and for all in the United States. |

# How Much of This Story is True?

## Location

There are two literal staircases in this story. The first is the outdoor staircase of more than 100 steps, sometimes known as the "freedom stairway," located in Ripley, Ohio. Some of the risers are stones set into the earth, but a new wooden staircase replaces the original stairway as one climbs higher to the Rankin House.

The second set of steps can be found in an attic of The Signal House Bed and Breakfast on Front Street in Ripley. The Signal House was built sometime in the 1830's, a few doors down from the house where Lowry boarded with the McNishes. No one is really sure what the attic steps were originally built for, but there is speculation that they might have been used by those who wished to send signals to the Rankins on the hill. In this story, the steps become metaphors—one set for the struggle of the fugitive slave to reach freedom; the other, for the risks taken by those who helped them.

## Events

Most of the events in this story are based upon actual events reported in Adam Lowry Rankin's *Autobiography* and/or in historical accounts of the town of Ripley, Ohio. I have taken some liberty with the dates on which several of the events occurred in order to work them into the framework of the story. For example, Peter Driscol's slaves were reported as having escaped in 1841, rather than in 1834 according to my story.

Also, at least one source sets Eliza's crossing of the icy Ohio River in the winter of 1838, as historical records indicate that the river was thoroughly iced over then. Another source indicates that the crossing may have taken place in the late 1840's. Most believe that the crossing took place at or near Ripley, however, as it did in this story. In some accounts, slave catcher Chancy Shaw assists Eliza out of the river and sends her on to safety with the Rankins.

Cross-dressing as a disguise for escaping slaves was apparently common, as related in several slave narratives in William Still's *The Underground Railroad*. The account of Rev. Rankin's disguise as a woman can be found in Eliese Stiver's book *Ripley, Ohio: Its History and Families*. A similar account was published in the *Boston Transcript*, Boston, Mass. in 1895 by Rev. S. G. W. Rankin, brother of Adam Lowry Rankin.

That any Rankin would be willing to go into Kentucky to bring back a slave, however, seems unlikely in light of a remark made by Adam Lowry Rankin in his *Autobiography*. Lowry relates that in 1837 he was asked to assist a man hired to go to Kentucky and escort several slaves to Canada. Lowry responded: "I promptly declined to have anything to do with any attempt whatever to go into a slave state to either induce the slaves to run away or help them there to get away . . . . In a free state I was most willing to do all in my power to assist a fugitive from slavery. In Kentucky the penalty for such activity was certain to be twenty-one years in the penitentiary. I urged him to give up the attempt."

In all probability, a third party, with the aid of the Rankins, helped Eliza to carry out the rescue of her children (see Chapter 22 of Ann Hagedorn's *Beyond the River*).

# *Characters*

The famous Beechers, including Harriett, reportedly were visitors to the Rankins' church and home. Several reports document that Harriett did indeed hear about the story of Eliza's crossing the icy Ohio River from the Rankins, and she included the anecdote in her book *Uncle Tom's Cabin.*

Ben Templeton was a boarder and friend of the Rankins. He and Lowry enrolled in Lane Seminary in 1836. Templeton preached his senior year sermon to a packed house at Seminary Church with "a grace and dignity of manner that was not excelled by any member of the (senior) class," reported Lowry.

Lowry studied at Lane Seminary under Calvin Stowe (by then married to Harriett Beecher). As an interesting footnote to this story, sometime in 1837 when Lowry was a seminary student at Lane, a fugitive slave went to him for help. As Lowry was ill, he asked Prof. Stowe to transport the fugitive to the next station on the Underground Railroad . The fugitive saved Prof. Stowe from drowning as they crossed the flood swollen Little Miami River.

# Questions and Answers About Slavery and the Underground Railroad

**1. When did slavery in America begin?**

The first large-scale enslavement of African people by Western Europeans began in the 1440s when Portugal engaged in slave trade with West Africa. These slaves probably serviced the sugar plantations in the Atlantic Islands.

The first African slaves arrived in Jamestown, Virginia in 1619. Of the 100 Africans taken aboard the ship that brought them, only 20 survived. Slavery was not legalized in Virginia until the 1660's, however.

**2. Where did the slaves come from?**

Some Africans were captured in tribal wars by other Africans and then traded to Europeans for goods. Others were captured (and hunted) by Europeans who then brought their cargo to the New World and traded the slaves to the colonists.

Africans weren't the only slaves in the American colonies. European landowners enslaved Native Americans and indentured Whites to cultivate plantations in the New World. For example, in 1730, nearly one quarter of the Carolinas' slaves were Cherokee, Creek, or other Native Americans. Because Native Americans consistently fought and escaped from their captors, labor problems increased.

**3. Why did slavery flourish in the South but not in the North?**

At first, slavery was legally practiced in all 13 Colonies in both the North and the South. The Massachusetts colony, for example, legalized slavery in 1641. Between 1780 and 1786, the Northern states either abolished slavery or allowed for gradual emancipation. Eventually, slavery flourished mainly in the South because of its agricultural economy. Southern slave owners depended on slaves to work in the cotton, tobacco and rice fields. Buying and selling of slaves at auctions was a major source of income for many. Consumers in the industrial North were always willing and eager to purchase inexpensive Southern goods, made affordable by slave labor.

### 4.  How did the "free Blacks" get their freedom?

Some "free Blacks" were set free by their owners. Others were able to earn enough money of their own to purchase their freedom and that of loved ones, and still others earned their freedom by escaping. For example, during the Revolution, some African American slaves escaped their owners and joined the British side in order to win their freedom.

### 5.  How did the Underground Railroad get its name?

According to one report (and there are several other accounts), the term originated in Ripley, where a fugitive who was being chased by slave catchers, disappeared so quickly that an observer said, "he must have gone on an underground railroad."

Another account holds that the term was coined in 1831 when Tice Davids escaped from his master who followed him to the Ohio River before losing sight of him. The bewildered master said that it was as if Tice had escaped on an "underground road."

However, many terms associated with the railroad came to be used in connection to the informal network of whites, Native Americans and free Blacks who helped fugitive slaves escape their bondage:

Agent or ticket master:  A person who plotted the course
of escape
Baggage:  Fugitive slave

| | |
|---|---|
| Conductors: | People who directly transported the slaves |
| Freedom line: | The route of travel for the fugitive |
| Jumping off place: | Shelter spot for the fugitive |
| Operator: | Any person who aided fugitive slaves |
| Station: | Safe place of shelter for fugitives |
| Stationmaster: | A person in charge of a hiding place |
| Travelers: | Runaways |

## 6. Why didn't the slaves rebel against their bondage?

They did. Resistance to bondage began when the first Africans were forcibly brought to the Western Hemisphere and lasted until the emancipation. More than 200 attempts of slave mutinies aboard ship are recorded. One of the most famous slave uprisings in the South was in 1831 when Nat Turner and five other slaves led a rebellion in Virginia. Eventually, Turner and his large band of followers killed more than 50 whites. Turner was captured and killed.

Some rebelled by destroying property, performing self-mutilation, poisoning their masters and committing suicide. Other forms of rebellion were less violent, yet still effective, including theft from the slave owner, pretending to be sick, poor work, and running away.

## 7. Why was the Underground Railroad in Ohio so well developed?

Before the Civil War, Ohio shared 350 miles of border with the slave-holding states of Kentucky and Virginia (now W. Virginia). A fugitive had only to cross the river to freedom. Also, during the 1820s, free Blacks who had settled in Ohio began to conduct raids into Kentucky to free slaves. These raids continued for decades. John Parker, a free Black who lived in Ripley, claimed to have assisted 440 fugitives on their way to Canada.

The Underground Railroad in Ohio reached its greatest level of activity in the 1840s. More stations existed in Ohio than in any other state. Another well developed Underground Railroad network operated in and around Washington D. C. Fugitives from Virginia and Maryland plantations were conducted through this network. Other hubs developed in northern cities.

### 8. Did all the slaves who escaped get help from the Underground Railroad?

Slaves sought freedom long before the development of the network known as the Underground Railroad. George Washington wrote in 1786 about fugitive slaves. Ottawa Indians were among the earliest helpers of fugitive slaves in Ohio before the Underground Railroad as we know it was developed.

Some fugitives stowed away on boats, and others walked the roads at night and avoided any human contact at all.

### 9. What motivated the abolitionists?

Abolitionists wanted to abolish slavery, but different groups had different ideas about how it should be done. Some abolitionists thought the slaves should be set free (emancipated) gradually. Others felt that the slaves should be purchased by the federal government and then set free immediately. Still other abolitionists, especially the Quakers and Presbyterians, were motivated by deep-seated religious and moral convictions about the evils of the institution of slavery. Some abolitionists, including John Brown and his followers, believed that slavery would only be ended with violence. In 1859, Brown led a party of men on a raid to seize guns and ammunition from the federal arsenal at Harper's Ferry. They hoped to use the weapons to start a slave rebellion. However, the plan failed and Brown was seized and executed. This incident helped to bring on the Civil War.

## 10. Why did the escaping slaves go to Canada?

No fugitive slave was safe from capture in the United States until after slavery was abolished. The British Empire, including Canada, abolished slavery in the 1830's, however, and made it illegal for owners to take back their slaves who had settled there. At least 20,000 former slaves had settled in Canada by the end of the Civil War.

Not all fugitives wished to go to Canada. Some went back to Africa to live in Liberia, which was founded in 1821 by the American Colonization Society. The idea was that in Liberia, Blacks could establish their own government and establish their own community systems. By the end of the Civil War, 14,000 Black Americans had settled there. Other fugitives fled to Indian Territory, or Oklahoma, where their descendants are known as Seminole freedmen or Black Seminoles. Still others went to Mexico and the Caribbean.

# References

## Books and articles:

Blockson, Charles L. "The Underground Railroad." *National Geographic* vol. 166, no. 1. (July 1984):3-39.

Burke, Henry and Dick Croy. *The River Jordan.* Marietta, OH: Watershed Books, 1999.

Coffin, Levi. *Reminiscences of an Abolitionist: Thrilling Incidents, Heroic Actions, and Wonderful Escapes of Fugitive Slaves.* Cincinnati: Western Tract Society, 1879.

Fradin, Dennis Brindell. *Bound for the North Star.* New York: Clarion Books, 2000.

Fritz, Jean. *Harriet Beecher Stowe and the Beecher Preachers*s. New York: Penguin Books, 1994.

Gaines, Edith M. *Freedom Light, Stories from Ripley, Ohio.* Cleveland: New Day Press, 1991.

Hagedorn, Ann. *Beyond the River: The Untold Story of the Heroes of the .* New York: Simon & Schuster, 2002.

Howe, Henry. *Historical Collections of Ohio.* Norwalk, OH: State of Ohio, 1896.

Lester, Julius. *To Be a Slave.* NY: Scholastic Inc., 1968.

Siebert, Wilbur H. *The Mysteries of Ohio's Underground Railroad.* Columbus, OH: Long's College Book Co., 1951.

———-*The Underground Railroad from Slavery to Freedom.* New York: Arno Press, 1968.

Sprague, Stuart Seely, editor. *His Promised Land, Autobiography of John P. Parker, Former Slave and Conductor on the Underground Railroad.* New York: W. W. Norton & Co., 1996.

Still, William. *The Underground Railroad.* New York: Arno and The New York Times, 1968.

Stivers, Eliese Bambach. *Ripley, Ohio: Its History and Families.* Ripley, OH, 1965.

## *Manuscripts*

*Autobiography of Adam Rankin.* Union Township Public Library, Ripley, Ohio.

*The Life of Rev. John Rankin, Written by Himself in his 80th year (ca 1872).* Durham, NC: Duke University Special Collections Library.

## *Websites:*

*The Freedom Stairs.* Selected primary sources from the Ohio Memory Project used by author Marilyn Weymouth Seguin.

http://worlddmc.ohiolink.edu/OMP/YourScrapbook?user=mseguin

*The Ohio Memory Project.* A collection of primary sources from archives, historical societies, libraries and museums that document Ohio's past from prehistory through the present. On

this site, you can search or browse the collection, and you can create your own scrapbook.
http://ohiomemory.org/

*The African American Experience in Ohio.* The Ohio Historical Society.
http://dbs.ohiohistory.org/africanam/intro.cfm

*Historic Ripley*
. http://www.ripley.k12.oh.us/Ripley/historicripley.

*National Geographic's Underground Railroad*
. http://www.nationalgeographic.com/features/99/railroad

/